Water-Gazers

Elizabeth Schultz

FUTURECYCLE PRESS
www.futurecycle.org

Library of Congress Control Number: 2017943592

Published by FutureCycle Press
Athens, Georgia, USA

ISBN 978-1-942371-34-2

To
My Brother,
Howard Shaw Schultz,
With Whom I Go On Sailing

Contents

AT SEA

The Fluid Line

In Palmyra, they draw a line
in the sand, and bombs explode
among the columns, restoring
them to dust. You hear that
the archaeologist's headless
body sways from a lamp post.
An arch, missing its keystone,
frames the desert's dry light.

Try to live near water. It will
keep you buoyant, said Thoreau.
You cannot draw a line in it.
Water redefines the shoreline
daily. In water, a straight stick
becomes a quivering snake.
Sand at the bottom of a pond,
a lake, a river embodies the waves'
flow. Down through the water,
the sun casts a golden net, rippling
over the sand, catching nothing.

AT THE LAKE

Baptism

Every summer,
the lake baptizes me.
Fish-like, feeling
my sheen, I slip
into the gleaming
basin. Water caresses
me, toes to shoulders.
How easily I might
stroke to the distant
shore, forgetting
the lake's frigidity,
my breasts' paralysis,
and the brazen jet skis
unzipping me.

Children in the Water

We watch the children
run down the dock.
The girl tests the water,
walking on her toes.
The boy flops out flat,
chortling with a splash.

In their new element,
the children turn shamans,
transformed into porpoises,
otters, seals. As sleek as
waves, they slip and
glide past each other,
circling together, kicking
up spouts, changing
green water to white.

They clamber up on the raft,
nosing each other forward.
Tickled by their shining
bodies, they leap like dawn.
They dance original dances,
exposing our lost selves.

Shopping at the Lake

No mall today, instead
the children tossed off
shoes and socks at random
in the grass. Stepping
toward the lake, skittish
as sandpipers skirting
this risky edge between
land's solidity and water's
liquidity, toes tingling,
tickled, then ankles ringed
by chill, and sand pressing
against their soles.

They stooped to see
pebbles—granite chips,
Petosky fossils, quartz—
an underwater counter,
objects of desire spread
out enticingly beneath
the lake's glass front,
all for the picking,
to be sorted, selected,
secreted in pockets,
transported to the city
for bottling and shelving.

First Swim

For Tim Crawford

All summer long,
we watched you,
swimming, spinning,
safe within your inner tube.

No one anticipated
the precise instant
when you kicked free,
splashing rainbows,
flailing forward,
beyond the snug circle.

Remembering our own
first joyous spurts,
we cheered you on
and clung to each other.

An Elderly Chinese Man Goes Swimming

He dazzles us in pale blue bathing
suit, enlivened by dancing girls
and swaying palms. His daughter
saw it on sale at Walmart.
She tells us he has never swum,
never been in lake or river.
He's also picked up sunglasses,
with chartreuse frames, and
a ball cap, its logo a happy fawn.

For comfort, he keeps on
his underwear; for security,
he is wrapped in a yellow
life-preserver: an exotic,
he seems to us, so long
familiar with the lake. It is
shallow here, and his steps
are tentative. Warned of fish
eggs and sharp zebra mussels,
his toes seek soft sand. A yard
out from the dock, caution
dissolves. He lets go, leans back.
Eyes close. He floats like a lily.

Elias Visits a Lake for the First Time

He wades in, oblivious
to the nasty parasites
causing swimmers' itch,
to the zebra mussels
with their cutting edges,
to possible scum from lawn
fertilizer, shampoo, and pee.

He wades in and reaches
down deep into the lake,
gathering armfuls of water
to splash across his chest,
gathering armfuls of water
to toss up into the air,
to watch it tumble down,
cascading, splattering, shattering
around him, into his mouth
in myriad bursting beads.

He wades in and shouts,
"I am a man of the sea,
and now I am a man of lakes."

He wades in and shouts
for his wife to bring the baby,
and when they come, he throws
bouquets of water over them,
blessing them in fluid joy.

The World, Their Oyster

At the end of the dock, the girls
spread out their towels and phones.
They slather themselves
in lotions, rubbing each other
until they glisten and purr.
They stretch out, glowing,
oblivious to the lake sloshing
beneath them, to fish basking
in the dock's shadow, to Icarus
splashing down by the island.

The girls talk their talk.
Cokes lubricate their gossip.
As clouds drift casually
across their backs, they slurp
up the heat, simmer with
the breezes, turning easily
on sensuality's spit, undisturbed
by passing dragonflies. Boys
gunning a motor might arouse
them, but at this moment, the lake
is their oyster, the girls, its pearls.

My Brother, Sailor

"O, Brother, what rocks your boat?"

We had our little boats,
my brother and I, and
they taught us to jibe
and capsize. We escaped
from shallow waters,
sailing into darker waters,
as far as Treasure Island
and the Gold Coast, but
no matter how long
the reach we were back
at the dock in time for dinner.

Married sedately, my brother
acquired a catamaran
with rainbow sails and
a flying trapeze. He sailed
in high winds, rudders
sizzling, rigging singing.
He put me on the jib, and I
scrambled through the lines,
hauling it in, as the cat ran,
churning blue water into white.

These days, he captains
a pontoon boat, capacious
enough for family and
friends on a sunset cruise,
out searching for cars,
sunk through winter's ice,
rusticating on the lake
bottom. Or on a wind-free
day, he parks this front
porch by swimming holes
and waits with patience

for us to slide into pellucid
water. Or maneuvering it
by himself in high winds,
hoping the motor holds,
he turns up Jimmy Buffet
and his Coral Reefer Band
and defies the wind again.

A Rule about Boats

Boats traverse water.
Boats thrash water.
Boats caress water.
Boats keep water out.

Defined by water,
boats, waterlogged,
sink or sluggishly
rock and roll against
a shore like bloated
sea monsters,
ready to expire.

To keep our light
crafts afloat, we keep
busy bailing boats.

The Voyeur

The girl paddles her canoe.
She goes along the shore.
I tag along behind her
as a shadow ripples across
the lake's bottom, tracking her canoe.

I watch her step over the gunwale
into the lake's clear water,
bend down to choose a stone,
focus her attention on one
among many. She skips it.

She can't escape me.
I know how she pauses, listening
to waves against the shore.
I stay with her when she drifts
across oceans and continents.

Years later, I know her better
as she sits on her shadow
and faces the computer's
rectangular components,
its small icons and low hum.

I am with her through the nights,
when she pushes off from sleep's
shore, paddling into the dark.

On the Drop-Off

On a morning so calm,
there's no strain at all.
I slip in the paddle,
glide it out with a sizzle.
Rippling forward, I scissor
across the lake's sheen.

The canoe moves along
the edge of the drop-off:
on this side, liquid turquoise;
on the other, opaque obsidian.
Maintaining equilibrium,
I switch left to right and back.

Dragging the paddle, I steady
my course between visible
and invisible. In the blue-green,
sun-lanced depths, my shadow
rises and falls, soundlessly,
running roughshod over
a landscape of wrinkled sand
and scale-encrusted stones.
It wavers across a ghostly
trout cruising among reeds
and bubbles. In a quickening
wind, I drift out into the dark,
over my head.

Snared

A birch leans out over the lake,
its roots land-locked, its head
of leaves swooping toward me
as I canoe along the shore.
Greenery surges in front of me,
massed leaves twisting, shining.

I paddle close in, crouch
to clear the birch's branches.
But these leafless lower limbs,
dark and dangling, scratch
my shoulders. I am snagged
by the living and the dying.

Hand-over-hand, I haul
myself through the tree's
heavy shadow. Untangled,
I move again, inhaling as
each stroke slices through
the lake's sheen into its depths,
exhaling as I lift the paddle
free.

Canoeing Along a Shore at Dusk

Dusk is the right time to mosey
along a shore in a canoe.
I glide across shining glass.

Beneath me, rounded stones
are settled in a mosaic
as established as Roman floors.

I pass the carcass of a skiff,
its outline sketched
permanently into the sand.

Gripping the sandy bank,
a birch tree tilts over the lake,
its boughs swooping,

its leaves, bangles fringed
in glittering light, tickling
as I paddle beneath them.

All along the grassy bank,
gentians, harebells, primroses
defy fragility through incandescence.

The sun incinerates the sky.
I backwater, turn against it
into twilight and the way I came.

In passing flowers, birch, skiff,
stones, I note each is encumbered
now by a little burden of shadow.

The White Boat

No one noticed when it arrived,
from which direction, or how
the lake rammed it stern first
into the sandy shore, the white boat
I paddled past summer after summer.

It marked my progress along the shore,
beyond the cedars' overhanging boughs,
before the patch of fringed gentians.
Years washed over its gunwales and bow,
and no one claimed the white boat.

It tilted uselessly to one side, swamped.
Smashed by ice one winter, its sides
collapsed and the slats floated away.
Each summer the white boat would be
waiting as I sojourned in my canoe.

For a time, its stern stayed high and dry,
a permanent ghost, until this summer
when waves erased it from the shore,
setting the white boat adrift to haunt
the lake, leaving me lone witness.

The Real Estate of Clouds

A land of clouds looms
over the lake, expanding
into mountain ranges,
diminishing to low ridges.
We devise cunning
cloud atlases and assign
geographic possibilities
to the lands of cumulus,
cirrus, and nimbostratus.

But clouds are as indifferent
to names as to boaters
and sunbathers on the lake
below. Clouds have lives
of their own and won't
be pinned down though
the lake tosses out sequined
nets. Clouds finger the lake,
their long blue shadows
stretching across the water
to probe depths. Carousing,
clouds flirt with the wind.
In cahoots with the sun,
clouds take on its radiance,
its startling iridescence.
Clouds cannot be measured.
We cannot package them.
They are not for sale.

Spider on the Lake

Sailing downwind over deep
water, sails pulling wing-on-
wing, the boat steady. A light
touch on the tiller, then the lull,
sails flutter, and we drift,
a feather on a mirror. Resting
on the boat's reflection, we
pass deflated spindrift and
a spider, spun outward onto
the lake by the dying wind
and near drowning. He staggers
aboard, seeking dry shade.
He shakes himself and folds
up, a small umbrella. On a day
this still, a spider and the boat's
quivering shadow on the sand
below urge me toward tasks left
unattended on shore.

Adrift

Windless and waiting
on a small boat, I exist unfocused,
abstract, drifting in the middle
of a plate flat lake like other
ephemera of foam and spume.

Until I'm claimed by evolving
clouds, opening petal by petal
above me into billowing white
chrysanthemums, bending
down, drawing me up among
their gold-tipped streamers.

Petals metamorphose into
vertebrae and ribs. I disappear
among long white bones that
soften, convert to feather quills,
inscribe the sky with rippling,
indecipherable orthography.

Until the main sheet stiffens
in my hand, and no longer
suspended among cloudy
alpha and omega, I yank it in,
cleat it down, and sail.

Aubade at the Lake

Crows startle me,
squabbling with jays.
Aroused from dreams'
dark quarrels, I lie, let
daylight lave me awake.

The lake laps against
my shore, flexing and
unfolding. It deposits
bits of opalescent mussel
on memory's edge,
turns over a dead crayfish,
its pink morphing into
pale blue. Silken water
caresses stones, slithers
forward, erasing tracks
of a fawn come down
out of mists to drink.

I turn over, sinking again
into sleep, but the lake
continues sending flotsam
and jetsam, and I must sort
the keepers from the dregs.

Wild Night

The night surged,
tormenting trees.
The lake charged,
rushing ragged.

Amidst such crashings,
such heavings,
my sleep snapped:
my halyards clanked,
my anchor dragged,
my mind unmoored.
Trees bashed in
my windows, and
the seas washed in.

Adrift, I imagined
hummingbirds serene
in their flickering.
Grasping at twigs,
they concentrated
on emerald essence.

Night Light

No twinkling light
by the bathroom sink,
I grew up mole-ish,
eager to tunnel the night.
Alone in the cottage
this night, hearing
voices, men rattling
mah-jongg tiles, I felt
my way, hand over
hand, one foot in front
of the other: down
stairs, out of doors.

Night's appetite,
immense, had consumed
cottages, hammocks,
lawn chairs. Lumpy
and heavy, dark was
wadded into tree tops,
crammed under eaves.
Shadows, irresistible
tonight, were absorbed
into hush, leaving a taste
of ash, a smell of pine sap.

Clattering continued.
Down by the lake, night
had thinned and paled.
The moon, full of ruckus
and bluster, was busy
throwing fragments
of raw light down onto
the lake's smooth platter.
They shattered across
the water, while the little
boats at their moorings lay
as still as porcelain chips.

Waiting for the Perseids

On the edge of a lake,
through thick night,
I follow a dull beam
to the end of a dock
where I stretch out.

The lake chortles around
me. Pines rise from the shore.
I conjure their sap, their
twisted star-pronged roots.

Overhead, the Milky Way
arches, emblazoned. The dark
swarms with bright seeds.
I am waiting for ejaculation,
for new seeds to burst into
bloom in this fecund garden
of stars. I wait for lustrous
petals to drift down through
millennia to be gathered
in my lap.

Bright Bird

In her swimsuit
of tropical flowers
and turquoise birds,
she perched, troubled
bowsprit, on the kayak
prow. Staring at her
own submerged
reflection, she clasped
her knees, tried smiling
at the lake's mirrored
perfection.

Seated behind,
her beloved rotated
the paddle, pulling
cautiously across
the shining water,
with each stroke
seeking to keep
the bright bird's
image from cracking
into fluid shards.

Sea Sickness

Nausea churning,
the boat swerving,
her salt level swirling,
sorrow swelling,
filling the sails,
as they discuss
their exquisite
childhoods,
new music apps,
Tasmania's best
birds, while all
presume her pleasure
in this flickering
water, this shifting
light on the sand,
as her smile
becomes a crease,
and the bilge rises.

Coming Storm

Gyrations in the air,
the pressure system's
felt presence, clouds
a shaggy mass, tousled,
gathering in the west.

We wait, watching
at the dock, the lake
transparent and still,
the waves' transcript
in the sand spelled out
line by line, gnats
pricking the surface,
and a telltale edge
of foam crocheting
lake to shore.

The boats are turning
now, the canoe bow
shifting north. Wind
frisks the witch hazel
leaves. Scrim after scrim
curtains the lake off
from us until draperies
dissolve the distant coast
in a rush of rain. Drops
reach us, flashing needles,
piercing, stitching us into
this process.

After the Storm

All morning from the dock,
we watched the billowing
dark on the opposite shore.
Consuming stray clouds,
the dark bulged. Towering
above the lake, it absorbed
the water's incandescent
blue and green, sucking up
the light.

Midafternoon, it blew
apart into lightning and
rain, roaring and thrashing,
stealing our power.
Lamplight vanished,
computers dissolved,
the fridge stopped cold.
We rediscovered candles,
checked old flashlights,
invited friends for drinks.
Ringed by flickering
lights, we played "O Hell."
Outside, night seeped in
to fill the storm's vacuum.

At midnight, holding
hands, our feet felt their
way back down to the dock.
The usual lights, pricking
out the opposite shore
in a glittering necklace,
had vanished, stolen, while
overhead, the chandelier
of constellations, sedate
and still, dangled in place.

Dalliance of Butterflies

In homage to Walt Whitman

A single monarch rises up
above the lake, pirouetting,
solo, choreography in orange
and black against fluid blue.
Conjured from air, another
appears, doubling color and
motion, twirling, twining,
looping, turning to rhythms
from distant forests, a *pas
de deux*, wings fluttering,
multiplying upon the lake's
surface. Lifting together,
circling, bending, they bow
to the long journey ahead.

The Island Exposed

1.

The island floats
upon an image of itself
in early morning mists.
It rises above its shadow,
adrift in fluid planes of
shifting pastels, mauve, rose.
This describes the island
in a photograph, abstract
and flat. I can try to fill
in the blanks while wondering
if 100 words or more
are worth one picture.

2.

We were three in a boat,
with one dog, somewhere
by the island when the fog
scrolled in, a density of
white, erasing us from
each other and all our shores.
We drifted in the hush,
muffled by plush silence,
listening for the island's
resonance, hearing only
the loon's cosmic laughter.

3.

A gale rising across the lake,
my small boat in irons
would not come about. Tiller
flapping, sail shaking, I was
sliding backwards into breakers.

Held the sheet tight, seeking
the island's lee, its calm and
shallow waters sloshing,
washing pebbles, where
the gulls stand unruffled,
facing east in all weathers.
But a congregation of winds
was gathered here, too,
and beating against the gale,
boom, my boat turned turtle.
I climbed aboard the carapace
to drift on my own island.

4.

Photographed from its
rock-ridged southern
shore, the island is a green
lump on the horizon, its
life, tangled in vines,
unfocused, underexposed.
The Grand Piano Ledge
stretches away from shore,
stones and boulders left
by glaciers, adored by fish,
hazardous for keels.
Here among the island's
stunted pines, warblers flirt
in a snare of berry bushes
and poison ivy. Scooting
in and out of the shore's
indentations, mallards claim
their niche in harmony with
dragonflies, water skaters, clams.

5.

Once, a hermit, bounty-jumper,
draft-dodger, philosopher,
claimed the entire island.

Once, my parents,
young lovers, skated
to the island, en route
engraving their names
in ice with their blades
in swooping cursives,
defying spring
to dissolve them.

Once, a buck swam to
the island, antlers held
high like a chandelier.

Now the island is owned
by the jet skis, cigar boats,
pontoons, fishing
boats, power cruisers,
catamarans parked here,
buddies, cronies, cousins,
uncles, neighbors posing,
bouncing in inner tubes,
swilling back beer, slurping up
leisure, glistening with creams,
digitizing their dreams.

6.

In this photo, the island
reflects upon itself.
It recedes into the mists,
or perhaps it is emerging.
The day is dawning,
or the evening is coming.
Only the dark island
stands out in this photo.
It is the right image to send
to a friend in doubt.

Halfway

Halfway between lake and
cottage, the small deck hangs
suspended among bushy
cedars and tall pines. I sit
in the midst of birds, minding
their affairs. Chickadees, jays,
titmice discuss the day, attend
their screeching young.
Hummingbirds whiz past
on personal errands. Beneath
the dock below, minnows glint,
a mandala of silver embroidery
evolving. On the dock, ducks
preen, settle in for the night.
The lake spreads smooth,
except for a breeze's light
tarnish beyond the dock. It
sighs as it touches the shore.

Often on such quiet evenings,
my mother came to this deck,
a pause between day and night.
Thoreau might have been
buoyed here. In the translucent
sky, a half-moon rises to erase
the last streaming clouds.
A passing herring gull pulls me
into air gleaming above the lake.
Behind me, in the woods,
a pileated woodpecker knocks
on wood for dear life. No mystery
or suspense, but in this moment
the plot thickens, culminates.

The Warming Lake

In morning mists,
simmering, shimmering,
the lake is a cauldron.
Fish, fried, float belly up,
flesh tarnished.

Too sluggish to rise,
waves swish a sludge
of cigarette butts and
condoms back and forth
to rim the shore.

We slather the children
against swimmers' itch
and sunburn, send
them out glistening on
bloated, plastic bananas.

The dog splashes into
the sludge, in pursuit
of a ball, comes up
shaking, drooling
with accomplishment.

Out deep, jet skiers unpeel
white water from the lake's
surface, screaming, roaring
against percolating heat
and the waves' disturbance.

We hear leaves curling
on the huckleberry bushes,
the crinkling of harebells.
Snails die in their shells.
The sun sears the horizon.

At night, we play "Hearts"
to shoot the moon and sleep
with every window open,
waiting for moonlight's cooling.

The Luck of the Lake

On a windless day,
the water in some northern
lakes is so clear I think
I still might drink It.

From my canoe, I look
into an aquarium's lucidity,
minnows meandering over
a slimy, quartz design.

Once crayfish moseyed
across the rippling sand.
Now zebra mussels have
colonized clam shells.

Round, black specks,
their eggs stipple rocks
like plague. I reach down
for a lucky, striped stone.

The canoe rocks giddily.
Small waves scuttle onto
the shore, jostling a plastic
array of flotsam and jetsam.

An underwater log turns
serpentine, and I skip
the stone across the surface,
wishing luck to the lake.

Moonstruck

We wait for our deity,
sitting on dock ends,
drifting about in boats,
all pointed east.
Disdainful, she delays,
permitting us no glimpse
until she is ready.

She teases at first,
tantalizing, revealing
a fan's gilded edge
above the trees' horizon,
before she will show
her full orb booming
into the wavering sky.
As if she would deign
to hear, we applaud,
falling into metaphors
and silence, watching
her progress up into night.

We should have learned
her sumptuous measure
can't be taken; she only
rises higher, remote
portal glowing in the night,
spinning a mercurial
bridge out upon the water,
teasing us to cross.

Voice of the Loon

Hearing rumors
through the summer,
we yearned for a sign
of the loons' return,
of the lake's revival.
Preparing ourselves
for the birds' coming,
we scanned the lake
by day and listened in
dreams through night.

Round midnight, the call
came, a mournful solo,
ululating over still water.
Warning or welcoming,
we couldn't translate.
In the western sky now,
a metallic moon gleamed.
Tapping this lunar gong,
the bird's sound rounded
the lake, resonating, and
in its unseen presence,
half asleep, we hoped
for a second coming.

Later, faithless, we switched
our allegiance to kingfishers
and swallows, omnipresent.
But still haunted by that single,
ghostly voice, we adjusted to
the loss of an immaculate world.

Summer's Last Sail

Rigging the little boat
by the dock, I prepare
for summer's last sail,
drop dagger board down,
attach rudder, secure tiller,
raise sail, cleat halyard,
these rhythms as familiar
as placing object after verb.
Hoist myself aboard, take
sheet and tiller in hand,
point the bow toward the far
horizon, check wind, chart
course, and sail again.

Sail over green water,
watch light ripple across
the sand, over the clams'
runic designs, sail on over
water crepuscular, gaze
down on an abandoned
anchor, the wreck of a car
driven out on winter ice,
cross the drop-off where
bass slip through lake grass.

Now into wide-open water,
waves flow, following
one another: a fluid script.
Sail across opaque blue water,
consumed and consumer
obscured: giant carp, Eurasian
milfoil, spiny water fleas.
I imagine lost cushions,
memories, songs, promises.

The wind rises. I hijack out.
Two loons, long imagined,
seldom seen, appear between
boom and tilting boat. Ahead
of me, skimming the water,
nodding, plunging into the lake,
they vanish, materialize again.
Will our narrative continue?

The Breathing Lake

Rhythm is the bone of the universe. —Unamuno

Used to ocean surf crashing,
my New Jersey uncle mocked
the sound of our inland lake
soughing against its shore.
"Lap. Lap," he said, describing
a dog drinking from his dish.

Calm days, plush water seeps
into plush sand and retreats,
seething, sighing. Small stones
and shells shift back and forth
without resistance, quiet dice
on a felt rim. Rougher wind,
and waves rip into the beach,
snarl, rage, foam at the mouth.
Retreating, they claw deep into
the sand, raking, rattling rocks.

But again the lake takes it easy,
its waters lapping, overlapping,
and I hear its breathing, its rhythm
coming, going, giving, taking,
as it polishes the bone of the universe.

The Written Lake

Only the poem is still
spinning lines on paper,
waves overlapping waves
overlapping waves overlapping

spinning lines on paper.
Sun rays shatter the water
as overlapping waves overlap
gleaming fragments.

Sun rays shatter water
into green and fluid gold
gleaming fragments,
suffusing the depths.

Green and fluid gold,
suffusing the depths,
spread rippled inscriptions
across the sand's parchment.

Spreading rippled inscriptions,
snails silently trail
across the sand's parchment
in the dissolving light.

Snails silently trailing,
glistening bubbles rising,
in the dissolving light,
clouds spill shadows.

Glistening bubbles rising,
the lake wrinkles
the spilled shadows,
the wind spraying spindrift.

The lake wrinkling
the manuscript's words,
wind spraying spindrift,
and a white gull scribbling.

The manuscript's words,
waves, overlap waves,
and a white gull scribbles.
Only the poem is still.

Leaving the Lake

Eighty summers,
I've left the lake for other places.

As a kid, superstitious, hoping
to return to find the lake's
shades of green and blue fixed
forever, catching my final view
for the summer, I'd wave from
the car's back window just as
we slid from the hilltop down
the rutted road, homeward bound.

Lately, I pay final respects,
standing at the dock-end on
my last day for the year, but
the lake, as always, just sparkles
and winks back at me.

Pastime

On this day, the lake, so clear,
reflected back upon itself.
At thirteen, on the dock, I saw
island and anchored boats,
duplicated in silver, drift close
enough to touch. Finished
painting my toenails, I wrote
out on the dock in red polish,
"Remember this day: August 24,
1948." Then, I reached across
to touch the opposite shore.

Years have passed, and I pause
often to stand before windows,
musing on oak leaves' swirl,
the collapse of clouds, snow
sifting down like code. I float,
high and wide, beyond these
windows. The opposite shore
always out of reach.

AT SEA

Land & Sea

When you sail,
both seem impenetrable:
the land a tangle of green,
the sea opaque blue.
You may guess worlds
of coral and opalescent fish
beneath the sea
and complex cultures
of love and loss
behind the massed brush,
but you'll never know
until you don mask and dive.

Sandspit

Arriving, immediately
we took to the beach.
Left behind were drought
and desiccated summer,
the cramp of airports
and the cemented earth.
Spread before us was
the sea, ceaseless,
anonymous, rimmed
with specific detritus—
stones, shells, feathers.
We mused over their
details, scrutinized
them for significant
shapes, stripes, spots.
Pocketing two or three,
we grasped at fragments
of forgotten infinity.

Porthole

Every morning,
she opened
the porthole,
and kneeling
on her bed,
did obeisance
to the day.
She looked
its unraveling
reflections,
its shifty clouds,
its luminescence
in the eye.
Every morning,
faithfully,
she focused
her camera
to frame illusion
within a frame.

T'aanu, the Haida Watchman

Carved in attention,
the Haida watchman
waits on the curving shore
between forest and sea.

An exclamation point,
he stands among knotted
cedar roots and tangled kelp.
Behind him, the forest's
dense mesh of thickening
green; before him, the sea's
snarl, swirling, curling blue.

Carved in attention,
the Haida watchman
waits on the curving shore
between forest and sea.

He anticipates the noise
of belligerent motors
from the sea before him.
He listens for the drift
of ancestral voices from
the forest behind him.
He has cetacean endurance
and the patience of moss.

Iona

Walking to the island end,
in a rain like penance,
flinging needles at my face,
clouds overhead dissolving,
reshaping as unsteady boats
drifting at sea, I approached
the beach where the saint had
landed after his raw journey
across the seas from Ireland.
Here, ridges of red marble ran,
streaked spring green. Inserted
among these hard rocks, tide
pools, microcosms of ease,
centuries of collected calm.

The Isle of Erraid

No errant footprint
marks this sand:
only the waves' imprint,
their perfect penmanship,
line on regular line.
Stepping foot here,
I trouble this clean text
with my copyediting,
disturbing the palimpsest
written out on this tidal
flat by birds, crabs, worms.

China Beach Comes Clean

Cumulus shadows cruise
across the hard, white sand
though Operation Rolling
Thunder no longer zooms
overhead, and Wild Weasel
Missions have gone. Beneath
the palms, Five-and-Dime
Rest and Recreation plays
in reruns. Lynda Van Devanter
is home before morning, and
the man from DaNang who
climbed into a wheel well
on the last plane out in 1975
is somewhere rolling dice.

The hard, white sand remains,
rinsed, scrubbed. A toy boat
dawdles on the horizon. Waves
scroll in, spin in, thin out, scrape
the sand clean. On this bare
parchment, a sudden scuttle
of crabs, a coconut husk.
My footstep intersects with
the waves' sloping cursives
before the restless message
rewrites itself, undecipherable.

Mangroves

Outlining continents,
ecotone of land and sea,
generating new earth,
absorbing tsunamis,
their seeds viviparous
and buoyant, their roots,
clawing down through
brine into soil, snarled,
twisting with snakes
and crocodiles, tangling
together crabs, shrimp,
oysters, and darkness,
releasing overhead a mesh
of shimmering salt-glazed
leaves, obscuring honey-
combs and the nests of
parakeets, mangroves
synthesize.

Water-Gazers*

On the pier
in the harbor of Guinea-Bissau
on the coast of West Africa,
where cashews are shipped
and cocaine arrives daily,
they wait through the day.

The woman in a long blue dress,
the man in a torn brown shirt,
the boy in untied tennis shoes,
they wait through the day

for a line to be tossed,
for a glance to be passed,
for an incoming freighter,
bringing news, for a small
cruise ship, bringing someone.

They wait through the day,
and tomorrow they'll return,
checking to see if the horizon
is still there.

*In the opening paragraphs of *Moby-Dick,* Melville
describes the phenomenon of countless people coming
to shorelines to look out to sea.

The Edge of the World

Dusk in this rusted
harbor, and adjusting
the scope, wiping
my binoculars, I watch
the life of birds on
the edge of the world.

Deliberate and delicate,
egrets, herons, shanks
stalk in the sewage
edging the shore while
sandpipers and plovers
peck and pull at
the muck. Among
rusting derelicts, a pair
of pink-backed pelicans
drift quietly, elegantly.

Hunched and hooded,
vultures sit musing in
a trawler's ragged rigging,
and above them, the sun's
red bulb incinerates
swifts, gulls, a falcon
into ashen silhouettes.
Awkwardly, great crabs
saunter sideways up
onto land, and a gray
gourami climbs out of
the sea, walking on its gills.

The Gambian Builds His Pirogue

Building your boat,
you will think
like the silver fish,
slipping through your hands,
like the little grebe
sitting on its reflection,
like leaves floating
in a small flotilla,
nudging the shore,
breathing with the tide.
Building your boat,
you will find your way out
onto the river, onto the sea.

Riding your boat, let it
leave the idling shore,
pierce the dark shadows
of mangrove swamps,
let it swim between islands,
drift silently across water,
be well balanced
when you bring in
armfuls of ocean parrots,
be filled with your gods,
your songs, and taro roots,
when you sail over the horizon.
before they come for you.

What They Had

It was what they had,
the children on the beach:
a small white egret.

Two of them stretched
the bird's wings out
between them, presenting
it to me, a broken parasol,
for a price.

The Door of No Return
in the House of Slaves
on the Island of Goree

In the screaming sun,
a polyglot crowd rambles,
selling and buying beads
and bangles, guides project
opinions on their bullhorns,
historians shake with
disgruntlement, fashionable
children dash in and out
of the claustrophobic rooms,
where the Door of No Return
opens soundlessly to the flashing
sea, while just a step down, waves
dash against a shore of ragged
rocks, and the horizon quivers.

Boat People

Bananas hang in the rigging.
No flag signifies nationality.
They sail port to port,
dropping anchor for a day, months.
She varnishes the teak.
He reads Maugham on the fantail.
A Pennsylvania quilt lies on the bunk.
Stuffed animals, a dictionary,
photo albums are on the shelves.
A phallic Marquesan tiki stands
on a red-checkered tablecloth.
On the morning a frigate bird drifts
in from the far surging horizon,
they look to the sea again.

Sea Stories

Sailing all day is fluidity.
You flow, come and go,
waves glistening, drenching,
rising, sinking in the great basin,
where corals bloom and dim,
where the sun fades, and stars
fall eternally, where the mutation
of clouds is incessant, where
narrative has no existence until
that day a whale demolishes a ship,
or you cross the horizon.

The Pacific

With less salt, less buoyancy
than the Atlantic, the Pacific
swells immense. Swells larger
than all other oceans. Swells
larger than all continents,
gathering waves and whales
and gyres into itself. Swells
in blue, cobalt, cerulean, indigo,
turquoise, azure, sapphire.
Swells with tides and winds
and currents. Swells with
cumulus clouds, rising loaf-
like above it, mirrored in it.
Swells over wrecks and reefs
and around archipelagos.
Swells into swamps, sewers,
city streets. Swells over the horizon.

Our Charts

On the charts, the islands
bloom, headlands projecting
into the seas like petals,
each island ringed by reefs,
barbed wire with gaps,
crucial if we are to sail into
moorings. At our briefing,
we mark spots for anchoring,
snorkeling, sites for black
pearls and restaurants we
can only imagine. We set sail,
our charts folded with care
like stiff linen tablecloths.

Each day, before sailing,
we open our charts, note our
place in the world of currents
and winds. We are aligned
by compass star. Agreed on
a route, we sail, the charts
near the person at the helm.
We check the charts' signs
for starboard or leeward
against markers in the lagoons,
call out names of bays, motus,
a vanilla farm. In time the charts
fray, are blotched with sun-
screen, creased, embossed
with coffee splotches, have come
to resemble our skin, ourselves.
They belong to all of us.

Crossing the Equator

Without ceremony,
we crossed at night.
Indifferent to new
constellations and
magnetic reversals,
we cruised over
the earth's bulging
midriff. Migrating
warblers or spiders
floating on invisible
silk, we slipped over
the unmarked sea as
we daily, oblivious,
pass over other
meridians, always
halfway to death
or resurrection.

Celestial Topography

My memory is littered with stars.
They glint and gleam at the edges
of all my pages. I turn to Tahiti.
First night out, lying on deck, mast
lights guided me up beyond stays,
halyards, lazy jacks, shrouds
into the spangled sky. The familiar
clusters of Cassiopeia, the Dippers,
Orion's Belt were off the page,
absorbed beneath the horizon,
or lost in glittering dust scattered
across the night. Seeking certainty,
I searched for the Southern Cross's
four stars, counting on this one
constellation to bookmark the dark.

Sailing Up the Coast of Raiatea to Taaha

Leisure is fine, so long as everyone has it.
—Virginia Woolf

All day we followed
shorelines, one island,
then another, steady wind
in our sails, going north,
a steady reach up through
the Pacific before slipping
inside an island's fringing reef.

We had no business here.
We were not cartographers,
not black pearl inseminators,
botanists, marine biologists.
We were neither selling nor
buying. We came to dawdle,
and then on a day like today,
to sprint, to ride the wind
like spiders, seeds, other
curiosity seekers.

Weather and the well-being
of each member of our crew
was daily news enough. Shirts
and towels dried on railings
while we weren't watching.
A red-roofed church on shore
beckoned to us. A frigate bird
passing by dipped a wing. Sunset
at day's end was headlines.

We rejoiced that someone
else had gone before us, plotted
the coastline, done the naming,

built the boat, harvested
the papaya and avocado we
had for lunch. On this day,
our only task was breathing
with the waves.

Dampness Is All

It's a condition. A malaise.
Without color or sound,
it creeps up on you at sea,
into pores and crevices,
infects your sheets and
the clothes you left dry,
saved for the city in your duffel.
It tastes of salt, has the feel
of fine grit, and at night
is your beloved's tang and
stickiness. It is insidious,
rank, lavish. You absorb it,
become it, exude it. Under
the sun's heat, it dissolves
into lace antimacassars on
your thighs, and when waves
rise up over the gunwales,
irresistible, relentless, it insists
you dissolve back into your
original liquid.

Nowhere to Hide

on a boat, except by keeping
eyes on sails, hands on helm,
keeping focused on charts, on
navigational guides: red, green,
square, triangular. No, nowhere
to hide on a boat except sleeping
late, napping, doing Sudoku,
crossword puzzles until it's
time to drink. Nowhere to hide
on a boat except in tasks: coiling
line, stowing trash, smashing
water bottles, cleaning the galley,
except, at last, alone out on
the bow, tasks done for the day,
there watching the bow slice
the green sea open, exposing
its heart of flashing white waves.
Nowhere to hide on a boat except
in the head, in your head, in your
bunk before sleep, scribbling
down your version of the crash,
reading a tale about a carnival
of outcasts wandering through
Quebec in the snow.

Ed Takes a Bath

Moored in a riptide,
our boat stood in the sea,
solid as a boulder,
though off the stern,
the sea streamed like a river.

Ed needed a bath,
and, heedless of tides
and currents, plunged
into this sea, rejoiced
in its rough cleansing.

But unlike his soap,
he didn't float. Scissoring,
he couldn't cut the water
and drifted, his head,
another lost coconut,
bobbing on its way.

It also happened that
someone turned to
the pulsating sea in time
to hear Ed shout, "Just
pass me a little lifeline.
I'm washing away."

On a Dead Coral Reef

Waves cresting, horizon surging,
swells deepening, spindrift flying.

Horizon surging, sloshing into the boat,
spindrift flying, sails taut on a breach.

Sloshing into the boat, vomit, trauma,
sails taut on a breach, currents compelling.

Vomit, trauma, the boat stymied,
currents compelling, the shore looming.

The boat stymied, we hold hands;
the shore looming, we crash.

Holding hands, we sit shivering,
crashed on a dead coral reef.

We sit shivering. We are a spectacle
on a dead coral reef. We collapse.

We are a spectacle, people staring on shore
as we collapse, as a tattooed man dives.

People staring on shore, dogs frolic
as a tattooed man dives, attaches a line.

Dogs frolic. We hold each other
as a line is attached to the shivering boat.

We hold each other, swells deepening,
the boat shivering, waves cresting.

The Scene of the Crash

No white crosses.
No plastic flowers.
No one died here.
Just a crash on a fringing
reef: a commonplace
in this archipelago.
Twelve days ago,
our common place:
hardscrabble coral,
blackened by motor oil,
here where the sea
scratches at the land.

Unkempt, like other
places distinguished
only by unwritten
memory. The wind,
echoes our previous
boat, crunching, crunching
up against dead coral.
Sailing past, a shiver,
as we wait for someone
on shore to remember
at last and ask, "Will
you be alright?"

Mooring

Whale ships were pelagic,
like albatrosses, left land
for years, sailing, sailing.
Our smaller pleasure yachts,
like sandpipers, kingfishers,
seek a shoreline as soon as
the sky signals purple.

Time to tuck in: either drop
the hook or catch a mooring.
All eyes and binoculars scan
the options: a quiet cove, not
too many other boats, one
free buoy, a good read on
the depth meter. Avoid coral
underwater, raucous neighbors,
sludge spewing from shore.

Choice made, deliberations
finished, we perform
the mooring ritual,
assuring easy sleep.
Boat hook for the buoy, or
crank out the anchor chain.
Let it down easy, link by link.
Crew at the bow signals skipper
at the wheel: ahead, back, right,
STOP. Hooked now, sit back,
search for the green light,
sleep in the cradle of the deep.

Anchor

At the edge of the world,
with the boat straining
and the sea rising,
everything depends upon
the catenary, the scope,
the set of the hook,
and the person checking
it in the night.

Ongoing

The sea throbbing, sunfish flashing,
sand seething, turtles hatching,

sunfish flashing, boobies plunging,
turtles hatching, frigate birds snatching,

boobies plunging, chicks gorging,
frigate birds snatching, iguanas watching

chicks gorging, sea lions loafing,
iguanas watching, crabs sauntering,

sea lions loafing, pups nuzzling,
crabs sauntering, sun pulsating,

pups nuzzling, air twitching,
sun pulsating, a shark circling,

air twitching, blood spreading,
a shark circling, a pup missing,

blood spreading, the surf muddied,
a pup missing, protoplasm adjusting,

the surf muddied, the sand seething,
protoplasm adjusting, the sea throbbing.

Oil Travels

The oil travels across
the surface of the sea,
a shimmering snake,
at the whims of winds
and currents, coagulating.

The oil travels across
the surface of the sea,
spreads out into a seductive
rainbow, glistening,
thinning into shining foil.

The oil travels across
the surface of the sea,
roils in the surf before
reaching rookeries
and mangrove swamps.

The oil travels across
the surface of the sea.
Dispersed by chemicals,
it keeps on roaming
just below the surface.

The oil travels across
the surface of the sea,
and no one sees it
sinking down among
plankton and shrimp.

The oil travels across
the surface of the sea,
feeding the starving,
sterilizing the living,
impervious.

The oil and the sea
will travel together
forever.

Re-Viewing Kate Chopin's The Awakening

She strips,
leaving a weight of white
petticoats on the shore,
and steps toward the sea
where it meets the white sand,
whispering and sighing as
the surf stirs up rusty-red glue.

Caressed by the sea,
she leaves Grand Isle behind,
sets her sights on deep-water
horizon and Barataria Bay.
In the novel, she strokes strongly,
stretching beyond the children's
calling and others' expectations.

She awakens to her own
supple body and in this poem
to sluggish turtles swimming
alongside her in the sludge.
She crawls through the waves'
swelling sheen, through
the shadows of birds, and sinks
with the dolphins beside her.

Voyeurism

I have contrived to be here
through complicated planning and
expense: suspended in mid-ocean.

Facedown and cold, through
a dim scrim, a voyeur, I gaze
down on new worlds, geologies
in coral, finned birds. They flit
into canyons, grottoes, circle
turquoise boulders, pass
through phosphorescent forests.

Cradled by currents, I view
giant clams and sea cucumbers,
siphoning, consuming, excreting.
On the reef, I appear another
nonchalant drifter, but with diatoms
clicking against my pulse, and
lusting, I imagine ejaculations,
assassinations, resurrections.

Butterfly Bay Beach

"Full fathom five thy father lies." —Shakespeare

A drowned mountain,
the island keeps only its peak
above the fluctuating tide.
Among crackled boulders,
its forests gasp with green.

In the hoop pines, cockatoos
gather in a raft of gaiety,
shrieking, "Bloody Murder,"
and the gullies stay lit
with flickering butterflies.

In the surrounding sea, rays
flash like silver spaceships
in the moonlight. Turtles haunt
these waters, placid ghosts
lifting their heads above the waves.

On the beach, we kick up
the bones of coral, scavenge
bits of carapace and shell,
breathe easy, away from
the boat's close sarcophagus.

The Outer Reef

Embracing the islands,
the shimmering surf,
swooping in from the sea,
surging, curling white waves,
rimming the islands, fringing
the islands, slamming against
reefs, nourishing reefs.
The outer reefs fecund and
growing, swelling in place,
spawning, proliferating,
always pulverized by the sea,
the last defense, challenged
by plastic, by chemicals,
converted to skeletal acres,
empires of calciferous algae.
Booming, the outer reefs
surviving, thriving, myriads
emerging, metropolises
of sponges, urchins, eels,
wrasses, grasses, sharks,
angel fish, devil fish, parrot
fish, clams, turtles, multitudes
out on the fringing reef:
not an oceanic decoration,
not a tourist destination.

Snorkeling

We come, interlopers, masked
and flippered. Arms out, we
fly in, buoyed on the sea's swell,
to gaze down upon these dense
and subtle reefs. We float above
them, absorb their light-stained
canyons, their coral forests,
their multitudinous denizens.
We kick through them, stir up
chartreuse, turquoise, fuchsia
metamorphosing into azure.

It is too dazzling, too subtle.
We cannot name these shapes
or colors. We cannot see these
faces, look into any eyes.
They wriggle into crevices,
curve into shadows, dissolve.
Plenitude confounds us.
Why? Why so many? Why so
much? The parrot fish gnaws
on algae and spits out sand,
anemones cradle clown fish,
and clown fish feed anemones.

Touchy-Feely

I stroll the beach,
breathing light. Air
is roused to give
me passage, and sand
sighs, accepting
my imprint. Touch is
one-on-one. I finger
a tidal pool, stir up
ghostly nudibranchs.
My mirrored face stirs,
splinters. Touch and
be touched in return.
Though cactus, poison
apple, moray eel insist,
"Noli me tangere,"
a bivalve's lavender
satin and a seal's glossy
pelt encourage stroking.
So a feeling universe
invites me everywhere
to keep in touch.

Jellyfish

Their tentacles out behind,
they just go with the flow.
The hippies of the sea,
they glide about cloud-like,
in costumes, gossamer and
sequined. Electrically
charged, they pulsate ahead,
all aquiver in Day-Glo. Any
new current is compulsory.
Smitten with the tide, they
wash up, wasting like damp
paste on stony shores, opaque,
impossible to see through.

The Vulnerability of Big Animals

Buoyed by the tide,
she drifted, directionless.
Again and again,
we saw her spout,
a fluttering handkerchief
in the middle of the bay.
In the day's last light,
she waved her fins
like silver semaphores.
Have we always been
so helpless?

Conversations with Whales

Gaze into the Pacific's opalescent pools,
cetacean nurseries, and, says Melville,
young whales, still umbilically attached
to innocence, gaze back.

Off the coast of Newfoundland, tap
a tune on the hull of your wooden boat
and whales nuzzle alongside,
clicking and spouting off.

Sail on edge among the Whitsundays,
with the keel strumming beneath you,
and a trio of whales arch together above
the waves, spraying arias about them.

Sleep in the cradle of the deep,
and whales snuffle up to your pillow,
their fish-breath fetid, their heaving
dreams as inscrutable as yours.

Echo Harbor

In Echo Harbor,
twilight hovers in a hammock
hung between day and night.

The sea relaxes, and the sky
lays out tinted linen sheets,
somewhat rumpled, across its surface.

Each island floats above its dream.
Heaped rocks and trees ride easy as
swaying howdahs on their light images.

Even the gull's throwaway down
casts a luminous shadow, until
it is absorbed by the darkening tide.

A Collection of Shells

Knowing summer inland lakes
with embracing shores,
we hadn't dreamed of ocean.
Now in the family car,
on our only family holiday,
away from winter, driving
toward Sanibel, my brother
and I stopped bickering
at Mammoth Cave. Smitten
by stalactites, we prepared
to be overwhelmed by wonders.
Christmas became unnecessary.

Quick into our bathing suits,
my brother dashed to the surf,
crazy, splashed up a frenzy.
Stepping into soft white sand,
I paused, enraptured by a horizon
that could slice sea from sky.
I turned to watch the sand funnel
into dark hollows behind my heels
and focused on the shells
clustered in bracelets and necklaces
on the shore's long tidal lines.
These I would name and keep.

We searched together, then,
my brother and I, competing
in discoveries and delight,
creating a collection to take
home, to line up on cotton in
a box, to closet away for years.
In my mind, I unpack them,
coquina, scallop, angel wing,

coolie cap, wondering how long
the sea will shell out
so capaciously, wondering
who cares for these shells now.

Children (K)Now

For Hillary, Timmy, Mallory, Aidan, Lucy

A great aunt, watching on
the sidelines, I see how
they glow and grow,
while greenhouse gases trap
heat near the earth's surface.
They do not do without
a choice of breakfast cereals
and velvet treasure boxes,
while the human population pours
CO_2 into the atmosphere faster
than it can be absorbed.
They race around on razor
scooters and are whizzes
with their handheld gizmos,
while oceans acidify and seas rise,
while reefs and glaciers disappear.
Abracadabra, they conjure magic
and appreciate mythology,
while deserts and wildfires rage.
They mind their manners and,
in her presence, mind their great aunt,
while a million species go extinct.
They are so lovely and so sure,
and though there's been enough
of steady loving, the children do
not sleep well and weep for the loss
of stars in their bright nights.

The Story of a Crash

The ancient mariner, again
and again, at a bar in
Kansas, I tell the story
of our crash, remembering
how the swells rose
to become the horizon,
at a Michigan restaurant,
how the waves washed
across us, in New Year's
letters, how mists erased
the islands' outlines.

In my sleep, stymied
in the current, Plato's
forward surging motion
thwarted, we drift.
A boat crunches against
a dead coral reef, and
my fellow immigrants
in stiff shoes, their long
dresses weighted with
sea water, the ship breaks
beneath them. Margaret
Fuller clutches her baby.
On the shore, no one sees
us. No Polynesian comes
on board, asking for
a snorkel mask.

Coming Clean

So, on the first warm day,
the farmer's wife released
the burl of heavy hair, knotted
at her neck. Washed in
spring water, the clump
of winter grievances spilled
open. High up on a ladder
fanning her hair out to air
across the barn roof, she flew.

Encrusted Odysseus came
to Phaecia and was bathed.
He shed salt scales and residual
vanities. Retaining barnacles
of memories, clinging to visions
of men lost, of a son and wife
in distant Ithaca, he was refreshed
enough to sing them all into story.

Naked in these sea-born hot
springs, womb warm, I floated.
Oppressions of long underwear
and a long romance, I stripped
off at the rocky edge and drifted.
Spread out below, oceanic islands
multiplied in mists. My breasts
rose in the yeasty water, and
floating, I turned to see two deer,
messengers, signaling the way
back to land.

Ongoing

With wildness a domesticated green
outside my window, I read
on my comfortable couch, aware
that beyond the Great Chain of Being
and without benefit of myth or symbol,
bird and beast go on cackling and
growling in the Ngorogoro Crater.
I know, too, that the sun makes its daily
journey across the sky above the pueblos,
and that once a year, in a fabulous fling,
the Kenutu corals ejaculate into
the tumultuous and spermy spray
by the light of the moon.

The Echocardiogram

Lying in the dark room, cast up
on a gurney, the echocardiogram
records my heart's gurgling grammar.
Tidal waters rise, recede. Rise up
and over, basins spilling, filling, quiver
with seaweed. Small translucent fish,
mussels tremble. I count one-to-eight,
waves slosh in, out, inflate, deflate.
After the last sail, the last snorkel,
comes the last breath, beyond waves
and the palpitating tide. Shallow, slow,
a sigh, a new language altogether.

Acknowledgments

I am grateful to the editors of the journals where some of the poems in this collection have been previously published:

About Place Journal: "T'aanu, the Haida Watchman"
Blue Monday: "What They Had"
Far Off Places: "The Edge of the World"
Legends: Summer Edition: "Children in the Water," "Elias Visits a Lake," "Luck of the Lake," "Off Path," "The World, Their Oyster"
The Maynard: "Snared"
New Mexico Poetry Review: "The Voyeur," "The Written Lake"
Open Palm Print: "Canoeing Along a Shore at Dusk," "Coming Storm"
Panorama: The Journal of Intelligent Travel: "Water-Gazers"
Pine + Basil Literary Arts Journal: "The Gambian Builds His Pirogue"
Pinyon Review: "Re-Viewing Kate Chopin's *The Awakening*"

Cover photograph by the author; cover and interior book design by Diane Kistner; Fournier MT text and titling

About FutureCycle Press

FutureCycle Press is dedicated to publishing lasting English-language poetry books, chapbooks, and anthologies in both print-on-demand and Kindle ebook formats. Founded in 2007 by long-time independent editor/publishers and partners Diane Kistner and Robert S. King, the press incorporated as a nonprofit in 2012. A number of our editors are distinguished poets and writers in their own right, and we have been actively involved in the small press movement going back to the early seventies.

The FutureCycle Poetry Book Prize and honorarium is awarded annually for the best full-length volume of poetry we publish in a calendar year. Introduced in 2013, our Good Works projects are anthologies devoted to issues of universal significance, with all proceeds donated to a related worthy cause. Our Selected Poems series highlights contemporary poets with a substantial body of work to their credit; with this series we strive to resurrect work that has had limited distribution and is now out of print.

We are dedicated to giving all of the authors we publish the care their work deserves, making our catalog of titles the most diverse and distinguished it can be, and paying forward any earnings to fund more great books.

We've learned a few things about independent publishing over the years. We've also evolved a unique, resilient publishing model that allows us to focus mainly on vetting and preserving for posterity poetry collections of exceptional quality without becoming overwhelmed with bookkeeping and mailing, fundraising activities, or taxing editorial and production "bubbles." To find out more about what we are doing, come see us at www.futurecycle.org.

The FutureCycle Poetry Book Prize

All full-length volumes of poetry published by FutureCycle Press in a given calendar year are considered for the annual FutureCycle Poetry Book Prize. This allows us to consider each submission on its own merits, outside of the context of a contest. Too, the judges see the finished book, which will have benefitted from the beautiful book design and strong editorial gloss we are famous for.

The book ranked the best in judging is announced as the prize-winner in the subsequent year. There is no fixed monetary award; instead, the winning poet receives an honorarium of 20% of the total net royalties from all poetry books and chapbooks the press sold online in the year the winning book was published. The winner is also accorded the honor of being on the panel of judges for the next year's competition; all judges receive copies of all contending books to keep for their personal library.

www.ingramcontent.com/pod-product-compliance
Lightning Source LLC
Chambersburg PA
CBHW072357090426
42741CB00012B/3064